Post Traumatic Stress Survivors Anonymous

LILY PAYTON

BALBOA.
PRESS

A DIVISION OF HAY HOUSE

Copyright © 2018 Lily Payton.

Interior Graphics/Art Credit: Meghan Morier

All rights reserved. No part of this book may be used or reproduced by any means, graphic, electronic, or mechanical, including photocopying, recording, taping or by any information storage retrieval system without the written permission of the author except in the case of brief quotations embodied in critical articles and reviews.

This book is a work of non-fiction. Unless otherwise noted, the author and the publisher make no explicit guarantees as to the accuracy of the information contained in this book and in some cases, names of people and places have been altered to protect their privacy.

Balboa Press books may be ordered through booksellers or by contacting:

Balboa Press
A Division of Hay House
1663 Liberty Drive
Bloomington, IN 47403
www.balboapress.com
1 (877) 407-4847

Because of the dynamic nature of the Internet, any web addresses or links contained in this book may have changed since publication and may no longer be valid. The views expressed in this work are solely those of the author and do not necessarily reflect the views of the publisher, and the publisher hereby disclaims any responsibility for them.

The author of this book does not dispense medical advice or prescribe the use of any technique as a form of treatment for physical, emotional, or medical problems without the advice of a physician, either directly or indirectly. The intent of the author is only to offer information of a general nature to help you in your quest for emotional and spiritual well-being. In the event you use any of the information in this book for yourself, which is your constitutional right, the author and the publisher assume no responsibility for your actions.

Any people depicted in stock imagery provided by Getty Images are models, and such images are being used for illustrative purposes only.
Certain stock imagery © Getty Images.

Print information available on the last page.

ISBN: 978-1-9822-1163-9 (sc)
ISBN: 978-1-9822-1161-5 (hc)
ISBN: 978-1-9822-1162-2 (e)

Library of Congress Control Number: 2018910689

Balboa Press rev. date: 10/03/2018

Contents

Preface..xi

PTSSA Recovery based on the 12 Steps of
Alcoholics Anonymous...................................xiii

The 12 Steps of Alcoholics Anonymous xv

   1. My Story 1

   2. Step One 11

   3. Step Two..13

   4. Step Three 15

   5. Step Four 19

   6. Step Five 23

   7. Step Six 29

   8. Step Seven 31

   9. Step Eight 61

  10. Step Nine 63

  11. Step Ten..65

  12. Step Eleven 71

  13. Step Twelve 73

Suggested Reading..75

This book is not intended as a substitute for the medical advice of physicians. The reader should regularly consult a physician in matters relating to his/her health and particularly with respect to any symptoms that may require diagnosis or medical attention.

This book is dedicated to trauma survivors everywhere.

Preface

Writing a book was the farthest thing from my mind. But as I was healing from my recent hospitalization I was doing a lot of meditation. It's been said that praying is talking to God and meditation is listening to God. Every time I meditated a voice calmly stated to me, "You need to write a book." "You need to write all this down and write a book." I couldn't ignore what I knew was divine guidance. I felt overwhelmed at the prospect of putting my life out there in such a public way. I told God if He wanted me to do this I needed His help. I couldn't do it alone. After that the words flowed out of me and the result is this book.

PTSSA Recovery based on the 12 Steps of Alcoholics Anonymous

1. We admitted we were powerless over our past traumas, that our lives had become unmanageable.

2. Came to believe that a Power greater than ourselves could restore us to sanity.

3. Made a decision to turn our will and our lives over to the care of God as we understood Him.

4. Made a searching and fearless moral inventory of ourselves.

5. Admitted to God, to ourselves, and to another human being the exact nature of our wrongs.

6. Were entirely ready to have God remove all these negative survival skills, one at a time.

7. Humbly asked God to remove our negative survival skills.

8. Made a list of all persons we had harmed, and became willing to make amends to them all.

9. Made direct amends to such people wherever possible, except when to do so would injure them or others.

10. Continued to take personal inventory and when we were wrong promptly admitted it.

11. Sought through prayer and meditation to improve our conscious contact with God as we understood Him, praying only for knowledge of His will for us and the power to carry that out.

12. Having had a spiritual awakening as the result of these steps, we tried to carry this message to trauma survivors, and to practice these principles in all our affairs.

The 12 Steps of Alcoholics Anonymous

1. We admitted we were powerless over alcohol—that our lives had become unmanageable.

2. Came to believe that a Power greater than ourselves could restore us to sanity.

3. Made a decision to turn our will and our lives over to the care of God as we understood Him.

4. Made a searching and fearless moral inventory of ourselves.

5. Admitted to God, to ourselves, and to another human being the exact nature of our wrongs.

6. Were entirely ready to have God remove all these defects of character.

7. Humbly asked Him to remove our shortcomings.

8. Made a list of all persons we had harmed, and became willing to make amends to them all.

9. Made direct amends to such people wherever possible, except when to do so would injure them or others.

10. Continued to take personal inventory and when we were wrong promptly admitted it.

11. Sought through prayer and meditation to improve our conscious contact with God, as we understood Him, praying only for knowledge of His will for us and the power to carry that out.

12. Having had a spiritual awakening as the result of these Steps, we tried to carry this message to alcoholics, and to practice these principles in all our affairs.

The Twelve Steps are reprinted and adapted with permission of Alcoholics Anonymous World Services, Inc. ("AAWS") Permission to reprint and adapt the Twelve Steps does not mean that AAWS has reviewed or approved the contents of this publication, or that AAWS necessarily agrees with the views expressed herein. A.A. is a program of recovery from alcoholism only - use of the Twelve Steps in connection with programs and activities which are patterned after A.A., but which address other problems, or in any other non-A.A. context, does not imply otherwise.

My Story

I look to the right and a young doctor in maroon scrubs is talking to me. She tells me she's a neurologist and so far the CT scan, EEG, and EKG they've done are all normal. She now wants to do an MRI of my brain. I look down and see I'm in a hospital gown, on a stretcher, in the Emergency Room. I have an IV in my right arm. I look at the clock on the wall and it says 3:00. Is it A.M. or P.M.? I have no idea. I turn to the left and see my husband and daughter. I ask Scott, "What's going on? What happened?"

He tells me that we got up today, as usual, got dressed, and went to our regular AA meeting, like we always do. I was supposed to chair the meeting but he says I just stood there by the table. He asked me if I wanted him to chair it and I said yes. I sat there through the meeting and listened. After the meeting, my sponsee, went up to Scott and told him to take me to the ER. She said I kept asking her the same question, over and over again. She'd answer it and in a few seconds I'd ask it again. I have no memory of any of this, just sort of "coming to" in the ER. How does anyone not remember someone starting an IV on them, or putting electrodes all over your head and doing an EEG? Scott says I knew him, my daughter, and friends, but just kept asking him. "What's happening? What's going on?". He would explain everything to me again and again. The last thing I remembered was eating pizza for dinner the night before. Maybe there was something in the sauce.

All I did know was that it was very frightening to find myself in this position. I remembered everything from that time on, which relieved my husband because I stopped repeating myself every few minutes. I'm told it's 3 P.M. on Saturday. Now I'm asking myself, "What happened to me? Have I gone crazy?" It's so disorienting. I feel very vulnerable. They do the MRI of my brain, which I'll talk more about later, and admit me to the hospital for observation overnight to be sure I'm not having a stroke or some other neurological event.

The night was uneventful. My wonderful family was with me at all times and I felt very blessed to have them in my life. By morning, I felt more grounded. I have to say the whole event reminded me of the many blackouts I had in my drinking years. Here I am, 29 years sober, feeling the same feelings and asking the same questions. It's demoralizing and this time it happened without any alcohol. What's that all about? Of course, I knew what it's about. It's the trauma, AGAIN!!!!! The traumas I've been working on and healing ever since

I got sober. I find it interesting that at no time in this whole process did anyone in the ER ask me if I had any history of trauma. But no one did.

The neurologist came in Sunday afternoon to tell me the MRI was completely normal. No signs of stroke, epilepsy, tumor, or early Alzheimer's, and she was done with me. She told me my official diagnosis is "Transient Global Amnesia", a rare condition, seemingly harmless unless it's happening to you. I'm told it rarely reoccurs. I found this a little humorous at this point so I asked her what causes it. She says no one knows. Thank you mainstream medicine, once again, for your lack of integrative medical approaches. I asked if there was anything I should do once I went home and she said no. I thanked her for her services and kindness, and told her I knew what to do next. She said, "Oh, that's good, and exited quickly, never to be seen again.

It was plain that I had work to do to find out how this happened, and healing to do, to prevent it in the future. I also knew that I needed to share my story for others who may be struggling with Post Traumatic Stress Disorder (from now on referred to as PTSD) or who have been written off as neurotic or just plain crazy. So begins my story.

I was a normal adult, actually, an over achiever. I was successful in my field. I became a nurse, working for years in Emergency Rooms treating all kinds of trauma. It took a special kind of person to deal with the

Lily Payton

kind of things we saw every day, but we thrived on it. We all worked hard and played hard. You'd go to the bar too if you saw and treated what we did each night.

From the time I was a kid I had a "startle response", jumping at loud noises and yelling out if you came up behind me and touched me. Frequent nightmares as a child, resulted in my wetting the bed. I didn't dream as an adult because I drank to go to sleep. I was hyper-vigilant, always looking around, scanning my environment, sitting with my back to the wall so I could see everyone, and was also the "life of the party". I was very good at compartmentalizing my life. At work, I was focused and driven to be the very best. When I partied I closed the bar and looked for the after-hours party. Home late, up early, groping for my morning coffee, shaking off the night before and heading to the hospital to "mend the broken" once again. That was until it all came crashing down on me on October 9th, 1986.

By then I was a Director of Nursing, wining and dining prospective medical personnel to come to our hospital. The Prospective clients were having a great time. I was "controlling how much I drank in front of them" as I usually did, but they wanted, after our dinner and numerous bottles of wine, to go bar-hopping. I took them to my favorite haunt, saying to myself, "Be careful how much you drink, stay in control." I needed to be home by 9 or 10 P.M. as my daughter was coming home for the weekend.

The next thing I remember was waking up in my bed at 7:15 A.M. I staggered to the bathroom and saw my clothes on the floor, covered in vomit. I went downstairs. My daughter was sitting on the couch. I apologized and told her I didn't remember what happened after taking my clients to the bar. She told me that my friend, Joe, the bartender, took my keys and brought me home. She said, "That's all right, Mom, it doesn't matter." Those words went through me like a dagger. For the first time I realized how my drinking had affected her all these years. How many times she had seen me incapacitated or passed out from drinking. I went upstairs, looked up Alcoholics Anonymous in the yellow pages, and went to my first meeting. It saved my life.

I soon came to realize that stopping drinking was just the first step. When I had stopped medicating with alcohol, I was raw and vulnerable. The nightmares returned, almost always a dark masculine figure at the foot of my bed. I would wake up in a terror, barely able to breathe. One night I heard a sound downstairs. I started down the steps and froze half way down. I could not move. I don't know how long I stayed there but I never did go down. I ran back to my bedroom and hid in the corner for what seemed like an eternity. I had always heard about the Fight or Flight Response, but no one said anything about "Freeze", at least not back in 1986.

I was going to meetings but struggling with finding a Higher Power I could connect to. I was told it was important to find one if I wanted to stay sober. I had no use for the God of my childhood. It was suggested to me that I ask for willingness, could I just be willing to find a Higher Power. I said yes and asked for willingness every day after that. A few weeks later I went on a trip to Dallas to sing with a trio I was in. We had some time to kill so we went to an art exhibit. It turned out to be a hologram exhibit. As I walked from image to image I was thunderstruck. I looked at one figure and it was a picture of James Dean. When I turned a quarter turn, that same framed portrait became Marilyn Monroe. I stood there for the longest time, turning my head, changing the image from one to the other. It was riveting and mind-altering, or perhaps mind-expanding might be a better term. Something profound happened to me in that exhibit.

When I got home, I started reading about holograms, how they're made, etc. The most informative book was *"The Holographic Universe"* by Michael Talbot. I am eternally in his debt for sharing his knowledge. After reading that, I had a first time real spiritual foundation. The Baltimore Catechism, my childhood Catholic reader, finally made some sense. God is everywhere and in everything. If I substitute Light for God, I know it's everywhere, It depends on how I diffract that light that determines what image I see. There is no separation, only the illusion of it. It's all about perception and where I focus my mind. I did not feel alone anymore and I felt like I had a true sense of personal power. I had choices. I could decide which way I wanted to perceive my world. I thought I would be ridiculed for this view of my Higher Power but it was totally accepted, even if some in the group didn't understand what I was saying, they accepted my search and personal view.

Having a spiritual foundation, I was able to proceed to my fourth step, a fearless and moral inventory of my past. I began to write about my childhood, which I thought was all a big, loving Irish, Catholic, Norman Rockwell family. How hard could it be? Writing is a powerful tool that gets you down below the surface. Soon, intrusive images began flashing in my mind. At first, I thought I was just a pervert or something. Why would I see these sexual images? What was wrong with me? Then, one day the face came with the body part. It was my older brother. He was making me perform oral sex on him . I was so little. I was frozen in place, I could barely breathe. I was nauseated. What do I do with this information? For a while I just sat on it. I didn't want to talk about it to anyone. I felt very ashamed that this had happened to me. But at last I realized why I was always afraid of my brother. I started to get sick after that, sore throats, neck pain, upper respiratory and bladder

Lily Payton

infections. I felt weak most of the time. I had just started reading Louise Hay's *You Can Heal Your Body*. She talked about how your body communicates feelings you might be stuffing. There is no separation of mind and body. They are connected.

I tried sharing some of this in my recovery meeting but people weren't talking much about abuse then. They wanted you to stick to drinking stories but I knew this is why I drank and would drink again if I didn't get it out. One of the things I realized early on was that all my trauma feelings were bound with shame. In and of myself, I felt powerless all the time. I needed position and status to make me feel powerful but then that meant there were people "lesser in importance" than me. I knew that wasn't right but I felt caught in the cycle. The more I exercised my power, the more I seemed to step on other people. Because I had been overpowered, I overpowered others. But as I worked the steps I was able to start untangling this mess I kept creating. Most people said they didn't know how to help me with this. So I began to read books on abuse and do my own work. I do not recommend this approach. I think it's important to have a "sponsor", someone who's been through it and has done healing work on it. I knew I could work the steps on my trauma just as I had my alcoholism. I just changed some terminology to help me be directed and focused. There are no right and wrong answers to these exercises. You may have only one or two responses or you may have twenty. Just be as honest as you can and don't overthink your answers.

Step One

Admitted we were powerless over our trauma, that our lives had become unmanageable.

EXERCISE

This is a two-, part step.

Part One
In what ways have I been powerless over my trauma?

1. _____
   _____

2. _____
   _____

3. _____
   _____

Lily Payton

4. _____

_____

Part Two
In what ways has my trauma made my life unmanageable?

1. _____

_____

2. _____

_____

3. _____

_____

4. _____

_____

Step Two

Came to believe that a Power greater than myself could restore me to sanity.

EXERCISE
We're told that insanity is doing the same things over and over again expecting different results.

How am I manifesting this in my life?

_____

_____

_____

_____

_____

Do I believe in a Higher Power? If yes, what does it look like?

_____

Lily Payton

_____

_____

_____

_____

Is this Higher Power good, benevolent, loving, caring, protecting, nurturing? If not, it's time to find a different God in your life. Start being open to a power greater than yourself that is full of wonder, grace, love, and support. What does that look like? If you don't believe in a power greater than yourself can you make a commitment to just be open and willing to the concept?

Step Three

Made a decision to turn our will and our lives over to the care of God as we understood Him.

This is an action step for sure. It's about making a decision, on a daily basis, to turn things over to something or someone more powerful than me. The Serenity Prayer helped me with this step more than anything.

"God, grant me the serenity to accept the things I cannot change, the courage to change the things I can, and the wisdom to know the difference."

For a person who has had no Higher Power in their life for years, this is a daunting task. I thought I could change everything and everybody if I just worked hard enough at it, so to give up any control was terrifying and felt like a failure. To really look at changing the things I can might mean giving up something, which I find really hard to do. It might mean being willing to leave a relationship or a job, which can be very hard to

Lily Payton

do, and the wisdom to know the difference takes time, patience, and practice.

This little prayer is about learning a whole new way to be and live. But I don't have to do it all at once. There's no thunderbolt. It's about one step at a time. It's about learning how to accept things I have no control over. It's about walking through fear, and surviving on the other side.

EXERCISE

What can't I change in my world today?

_____

_____

_____

_____

_____

How do I feel about this?

_____

_____

_____

Post Traumatic Stress Survivors Anonymous

What can I change that needs to be changed?

What's the predominant feeling(s) around this?

Lily Payton

Suggestion: Do this exercise every day for 30 days.

Step Four

Made a searching and fearless and moral inventory of ourselves.

I have noticed many people in recovery become ill once they stop drinking. Many stop drinking and do the steps on their drinking but don't touch the deeper stuff. It began to make sense to me that if I didn't speak about what had happened to me I would internalize it until it made me ill. In other words, my body would do the speaking for me. I was also reading John Bradshaw's, *"Healing The Shame that Binds You"*, and doing inner child work. My inner child, always had dirty, stringy hair that hung in her face. She was always cowering in a corner. I did many sessions of connecting with my inner child, through drawing, coloring, listening, and writing with my non-dominant hand to give her a voice. I re-parented her and affirmed her until the images became positive. She looked happy, with clean curly hair brushed away from her face. She played outside and spread her arms out wide taking in the fresh clean air.

Lily Payton

EXERCISE

What does my inner child look like? What kind of family did she/he grow up in?

_____

_____

_____

How did my inner child cope with her/his life?

_____

_____

_____

What were my feelings?

_____   _____

_____   _____

How did I react?

_____

_____

Post Traumatic Stress Survivors Anonymous

_____

_____

How did I cope as a teenager?

_____

_____

_____

What were my feelings?

_____   _____

_____   _____

How did I react?

_____

_____

_____

_____

Lily Payton

How did I behave as an adult?

_____

_____

_____

What were my feelings?

_____   _____

_____   _____

Step Five

*Admitted to God, to ourselves, and another
human being the exact nature of our wrongs.*

I finally became strong enough to write my brother a letter. I told him what I remembered and that it was important for me to tell him my truth. Susan Forward's book, *"Toxic Parents"*, helped me write to him in a non-threatening way. I love my brother, I just needed to tell my truth and to set that little girl free. Two weeks later, I received a letter from my brother. He acknowledged the abuse and apologized for any harm he may have caused me. I was sitting on the couch and a sound came out of me from somewhere deep inside of me, something between a wail and a moan. My cat jumped on my lap and started kneading his paws into my chest. I cried like I had never cried before, releasing years of pain that I stuffed way down deep inside me. I am so grateful to him for his courage to tell the truth and help me heal.

One of the things I read about healing from trauma

was to find a safe place, physically and mentally. I carved out a nook in my home that was just for me. It was cozy, with a view of the outside. I started to consciously spend time there each day and just be with myself. I also started to meditate. I created a safe place in my mind that I would go to. It was a white gazebo with a beautiful white adirondack chair. I would visualize myself relaxing there, dressed in white, with a gentle breeze on my face looking out onto the water. After that I remembered many childhood sex abuse memories. I'm told that it's not uncommon for a child to repress these memories when your mind and body become overwhelmed by the trauma. My father was an untreated alcoholic. My mother worked nights and we were left with him staggering through the house at night. I had very few childhood memories of him but I remember I used to tell people I remember my dad picking me up from the couch, where I had fallen asleep and carrying me upstairs. I loved that memory, because it was one of the few times I felt my dad close to me. Imagine my horror, when the memory came flooding back to me, at around three years sober, that my dad had taken me to his bedroom that night, not mine, and performed oral sex on me. The memory was particularly disturbing because all the feelings I had felt then, returned, and my whole body felt sexually excited. It was in that instant that I had a personal and profound relationship with God, as I understand Him, I was feeling complete embarrassment and shame when I heard a calm, loving, voice in my head say, "I am here, Lily. I am with you. Don't be afraid." I sat and wrote the whole memory down. Even though I was shaking with fear, I put it all down. How freeing to finally be rid of this secret I had been holding in my body all these years. It took working a fourth step to understand that the embarrassment and shame were not mine to have carried and I gave them back to my father at his graveside. But it was two years later when I connected with the PTSD symptoms of how trapped I felt that night, a little girl around 4 years old, when my father passed out on top of me. I couldn't get out from under him. I could barely breathe. I was terrified. As a child I thought he was going to crush me to death. I used to have a recurring nightmare that I was trapped under a car and couldn't get free.

Soon after that I remembered one of my other brothers holding me down on the floor in my bathroom and grinding back and forth on me till he had an orgasm. He told me not to say anything and he went out and closed the bathroom door. That door always stuck a little. I was little and kept trying to open the door unsuccessfully. I was crying, panicked, and scared. I yelled but no one came. Exhausted, I laid down on the bathroom rug on the floor and cried myself to sleep.

My next memory that surfaced happened when I was about 5 years old. I was being held down by my brothers and orally sodomized by a Fresh Air* child from inner New York City, that our family hosted for two weeks one summer. Again, I felt trapped, had trouble breathing, and thought I was going to die. Once that memory surfaced, most of my hair fell out, I lost twenty pounds, and couldn't eat meat for several months.

The Iraq war was beginning about this time and I was having difficulty watching the news. It was the Veterans in the program who helped me so much during this period. They told me they understood my feelings and to hang in there, it would get better. They suggested that I turn off the news and stop reading the newspaper for a while until I felt stronger and more healed. They told me I was probably being triggered by the news back into my own violence. It was then that I realized that I had PTSD. I felt shame about that too. I felt like I was a weak person who couldn't just "pull myself up by the bootstrap" and get on with it. I wasn't "Jane Wayning" (based on Jane Wayne Syndrome) myself through this. Those vets told me how courageous I was to tell the truth and stand in my truth. How grateful I was for them. It became clear to me that trauma is trauma, whether in your cellar, or on the battlefield.

---

* Fresh Air Program is a not for profit program where you host inner city children for two weeks in the summer in a more rural setting

The feelings we had were similar and we could help each other heal. I did not feel alone anymore. Looking back, I had been in denial about my trauma symptoms for so many years, because I tried to control them with my drinking.

The most difficult memory, however, came a few years later. One of my brothers used to take me to the attic. It had been finished into a dormitory of sorts for the boys. There was a crawl- space for storage up there. It had a little latch on the outside of the door. My brother would lure me in there when I was little. It was completely dark inside. He'd sexually molest me, tell me not to tell, then leave me in there alone. There was no latch on the inside so I was locked in until he opened it and let me out. Besides the confusion and shame of the molestation, I was terrified in that dark space. I thought I was going to die in there and no one would find me. No matter how hard I tried or yelled, I couldn't get out. All of these assaults shaped a large part of my personality.

I was driven, a hard driving go-getter. I always wanted to be noticed. I was never happy where I was. I always wanted to move, to get ahead, to get out of where I was and be in another place. I couldn't wait to get out of my town and go somewhere else. I was restless, antsy, and never wanted to be alone. "The more the merrier" was my motto. It all made sense to me now. There seemed to be two sides to me. In my professional life I was fearless, rebellious, challenged the status quo, and relentless in my pursuit of excellence and climbing the ladder to success. In my private world, however, I tended to be docile, approval seeking, and needy. I couldn't seem to keep a relationship together. I would fall madly in love but once married, I started feeling trapped, bored, and would start "pining " for someone else, always in secret, never really satisfied with where I was or who I was with.

In recovery, I was just as rebellious. I will not find a God. I will not say the Lord's Prayer. I will not stop going to bars. I will not get a sponsor, etc. But the longer I was from taking a drink, the more I came to realize that the rebellious nature was covering up something much deeper in me, fear and shame. Shame comes from a root word meaning "to cover" and I had been covered up for years. My body language was stooped shoulders, averting eye contact, crossing my arms and legs, all closed body positions. It took a long time to heal the internalized shame from my childhood.

Step Six

*Were entirely ready to have God remove
all these negative survival skills.*

Step Seven

*Humbly asked God to remove our
negative survival skills.*

One of the major things that helped me was changing some of the words in the 6th and 7th steps of my program from "Were entirely ready to have God remove all these defects of character" to "Were entirely ready to have God remove all these negative survival skills". Defects of character cut right through me. I felt total shame just saying the words. Of course, at first, the shame was covered up with behaviors such as sarcasm, lying, judgment of others and self, isolating, blushing, polarization of feelings from numbness to angry outbursts. It took a while to understand that I already felt defective. As I did more work, I realized that these "defects" were all things that helped me survive the trauma I experienced. I started by making a list of all these behaviors and started working on them, one at a time.

This is where I saw so many people stop working

a program. They would make a list of their defects, ask God to remove them and say, "Okay, I've done steps 6 & 7, I'm finished. I knew it wasn't that easy. First I would recognize a negative behavior pattern in myself, (a major feat in itself), I would ask God to remove it. Then heaven help me, I would begin to see it everywhere. And I would ask others if they noticed it in me. Their candor was unnerving and humbling to say the least. So every time I was sarcastic, say, I would begin to stop it sooner and sooner, and apologize to the person. These survival skills, sarcasm, gossiping, swearing, lying, self-deprecation, etc. were really a form of violence. The victim had become the abuser, not only to others but to myself. It seemed like every time I let go of an old entrenched pattern of behavior, a memory surfaced. I was no longer covering it up, so it bubbled to the surface. The other reason they surfaced is that I had finally become safe to myself. I was no longer shaming that little girl inside of me and she finally felt safe enough to speak up, to know that she would be heard and honored. Remember, I had worked steps 1-5 by this point. It is essential to have a power greater than yourself in your life, to do this work. There were times when I felt suicidal. I never acted on it but I felt hopeless, defeated, and the shame was all consuming. If I had not found a Higher Power I would have imploded. The remedy for suicidal thoughts is "to talk them to death". Suicide is part of the abuse secret and carries its own power. When I talk to someone who is safe or to the group about these thoughts, they start to lose their power. So I tell people, if you're having suicidal thoughts, talk about it until it has no more power.

Lily Payton

EXERCISE

List my negative survival skills:

_____

_____

_____

_____

_____

What was I thinking?

_____

_____

_____

_____

_____

What was I feeling?

_____

_____

_What are the healthy behaviors I want to cultivate in myself?
List a healthy behavior for each negative one._

i.e. Every time I find myself gossiping about someone, I will say something nice about them instead.

When I catch myself trying to control someone or something, I will stop, breathe, and say I accept this just the way it is.

Lily Payton

Lessons in letting go, de-stressing, and meditation began with simple coloring ...

Lily Payton

Post Traumatic Stress Survivors Anonymous

LETTER TO INNER CHILD
A letter of long overdue self-love.

Post Traumatic Stress Survivors Anonymous

LETTER TO ABUSER
Written in non-dominant hand, verbalizing
everything you wanted to say to the
person(,) who hurt and violated you.

I suggest you share this first with a person you trust before sending it.

Working steps 6 & 7 showed me how much I had compartmentalized myself in order to survive through the years. There were three parts to me. Each aspect of my traumatized self had its own script, rules, and personality, if you will. It all depended on what triggered me as to what script and role I acted out. I call it:

The Trauma Triangle.

It consists of the Victim, the Abuser, and the Silent Abuser. Each aspect of the triangle has its own script, behaviors, and personality.

The Victim script: expresses hopelessness, passiveness, neediness, low self-esteem, approval-seeking.

The Abuser script: physically, verbally, emotionally, or spiritually abuses the victim, through physical violence, controlling behaviors, and/or isolating the victim from family and friends.

The Silent Abuser script: stays loyal to the abuser at all costs; keeps the abuser's secrets; will interrupt the victim's grieving process either by gesture or words to stop the truth from being expressed; minimizes the abuse.

As a child I was the victim for sure. Being untreated for that abuse I grew up to be an abuser also, as all untreated adults do.

It depends how the light, (the trigger of the abuse) is pointed as to which personality trait "jumps into action". There were many times when I would be saying something and part of me would be saying, "Shut up, you're hurting that person". But I couldn't stop. Or a part of me would be saying, "Speak up, this is wrong", but nothing would come out of my mouth. I'd sit there in silence. Or there were the times when I would side with someone on an issue that I knew was wrong but couldn't seem to say so, and instead would nod in agreement.

I wrote out these patterns and shaming tapes and challenged them, then wrote out a new, affirming tape for each one. It was very important to stop shaming myself, which was an ingrained pattern. Every time I'd catch myself doing it, I'd just acknowledge it. It was also important to play the negative tape all the way through, consciously release it, then say the new positive tape.

Examples:

Old tape: I'm so stupid, I'll never catch on to this.

New tape: I'm smart and know I'm just in a learning curve.

Old tape: I can't have that. I don't deserve it.

New tape: I deserve the best because I am the best.

Learning self-love can be hard work, especially if it wasn't modeled for you. Go ahead, get a notebook and start writing. It can feel uncomfortable, embarrassing, and unattainable at first, but I promise you it gets better and is worth the effort in the end. It is important to have a sponsor that is on the same page and does not shame you. If you have a shaming sponsor, fire them and get another one, today!

Shame

This is a huge emotion. In my opinion it's the leading cause of relapsing behaviors and suicide. It is overwhelming and very painful. Sometimes it feels like death would be easier. It separates me from the group, from God, and even from parts of myself. It tells me I'm bad and don't deserve good things. It causes me to blush, then feel anger because I can't control it. It causes my hands to tremble. I can't maintain eye contact. It rounds my shoulders and gives a stoop to my walk. I cannot truly love and be intimate because if you knew who I really was you'd walk away. So I walk away first. It stifles my creativity. I always wanted to sing but I couldn't be good enough. Even if you told me I had a good voice, I couldn't trust it because my trust had been broken at a young age. It's a deep hole to be in and there doesn't seem to be any way out. But there is. It takes work but what's the alternative? What do you have to lose at this point? Here's what I had to do:

Keeping My World Safe

My world had been unsafe for so many years. I had no boundaries growing up so as an adult I had no sense of your space or mine. Because of my terror when left alone in a place I could not get out of, I was constantly looking for touch which set me up for more abuse. I couldn't stand to be alone or sit in silence. I always had the radio or TV on. When I realized that I had been victimized it gave me a frame of reference for the first time. I could begin to identify abuser behaviors. With a group, a sponsor, and a budding spiritual foundation, I was finally learning to be by myself and not "jump out of my skin". I did not need to be around people who were controlling, shaming, or hurtful.

Setting boundaries, though, if you're not used to it,

is formidable. The first time I set a firm boundary my body shook. My mind could say no all day long, but to actually say no to someone out loud was terrifying. Let me clarify this. I was good at packing my stuff and stomping out the door, ending the relationship, rather than just saying no, or stomping out only to return hours later, crying and giving in, losing more of my soul each day. If you're beginning this work, it's important to do it with someone who's already done it. You role play it with them first just to get used to saying the boundary out loud. Even if my voice was shaking a little, my best boundaries were said calmly, and just stating my needs. As someone once said, "No" is a complete sentence. Setting boundaries in this manner keeps my power intact.

Keeping my world safe, can also mean removing myself physically from a situation or place and going somewhere that is safe for me. That means I have to make two lists: Safe Places and Unsafe Places. If I'm in a vulnerable state, going home and being alone with myself may not be safe. Where do you feel safest? Who do you trust? Reach out and confide in a safe person. Believe me, your list of safe people will change as you do this work. But it's imperative that you keep your world safe so some friends or relatives may even need to be crossed off that list, at least temporarily, until you've healed more. Some you may invite back into your life later, and some may never feel safe again. You'll know. Talk with your sponsor and trust your gut.

My Safe World	*My Unsafe World*
My 12 step meeting room	Barroom
My sponsor	My Ex's apartment
The pond at the park	Interacting with relatives don't believe my history

How do you know if your world is not safe?

1. Is a person continually entering into your personal space without your permission?
2. Is the person shaming you, putting you down, making jokes at your expense, sexualizing you verbally or non-verbally, attacking you physically or verbally, guilting or manipulating you even when you've asked them to stop.
3. Is he or she telling you they don't believe what happened to you?
4. Are you feeling off balance?

Lily Payton

EXERCISE

Sit down and be quiet for a few moments, breathe in and out, then think about what a safe world would look like in your universe. Write it down.

My Safe World:

_____

_____

_____

_____

_____

_____

Then begin to build it.

Write down what an unsafe world looks like.

My Unsafe Word:

_____

_____

_____

_____

_____

_____

_____

_____

Now start eliminating it from your world.

Lily Payton

It's okay for me to ask for what I want and need and it's important to me that it be respected. When setting boundaries, I keep the focus on myself, such as, "When you come up behind me and slap me on the back it scares me." This works much better than, "Knock it off!" But I have to remember that I cannot change another human being. If they don't respect the boundary I set then I have to make decisions. I no longer have to put up with "bad behavior" but I may have to leave the situation, the relationship, the job, etc. to be free from the abuse. One thing I've learned from experience in this work, is WHEN YOU SET A BOUNDARY, YOU WILL INCUR A LOSS. Be prepared, and know that there are necessary losses. Then I have to grieve the loss and feel my feelings fully through the process. The good news is: AT THE END OF THE GRIEVING, WHEN I LET GO, THERE IS ALWAYS A GIFT. Be sure to look for it.

Post Traumatic Stress Survivors Anonymous

TRAUMA HEALING RULES

1. When I set a boundary I will incur a loss.

2. There is always a gift at the end of the Grieving.

3. When someone is expressing or grieving their trauma, do not touch them unless you ask first and receive their permission.

4. Be gentle with yourself.

5. Don't shame yourself or others.

Grieving

Every trauma memory has to be grieved fully. One of the symptoms of PTSD is the inability to grieve. It is blocked by the suppressed feelings around the trauma. There are five stages to grief:

1. Denial and Isolation.
2. Anger/Rage
3. Bargaining
4. Depression
5. Acceptance

Elizabeth Kubler-Ross, in her book, "On Death And Dying", has outlined them and in doing so helped millions of people to be free from and to resolve debilitating loss. The emotion I've had to add to this process is shame. IN THE TRAUMA HOLOGRAM, SHAME IS BOUND TO EACH STAGE. As I go through each stage, and acknowledge my feelings fully, the shame begins to release and unbind itself from that particular stage. Shame release is powerful. It exhibits in many physical forms; herpes outbreaks (oral and/or genital)bladder infections, rashes, heavy makeup, provocative clothing, baggy clothing. The list goes on and on. Holographically, if I'm in my shame, I'm constantly wearing my sunglasses When I'm breaking shame, I would lose my sunglasses. I started buying cheap ones because I lost so many. If I'm in my shame, I find myself wearing a hat. If I'm releasing the shame I can't keep a hat on. I also drop a lot of things when I'm detaching from the shame. It used to really upset me at first until I realized it was it was part of the healing. Now I just laugh and thank God for the positive message. The hologram is the combination of the conscious and collective unconscious language, (the nonverbal language), that is always communicating with us and trying to connect with us. Keeping a daily journal is very helpful in healing. I begin to see old patterns, old tapes, and as I progress, I begin to see new healthy patterns of how I'm breaking and releasing shame and developing new, healthy tapes in my life.

Denial

Denial is an entrenched survival skill to prevent one from overwhelming feelings and memories. Denial coupled with the shame of the traumatic event often leads to addictions. The addictive process is a medication that temporarily soothes the anxiety, temporarily relieves the stress, and allows one to breathe, when having been triggered back into the trauma. Anything can become an addiction. Here are just a few:

Alcohol and Drugs
Food
Anorexia and/or Bulimia
Bullying
Creating excessive debt
Gambling
Sex addiction
Sexually Anorexic
Love Addiction
Pornography
Shopping
Smoking
Video Games
Excessive TV, internet
Excessive Sleeping
Excessive working
Excessive exercising

Lily Payton

Excessive risk taking
Cutting-Self Mutilation
Codependency
Stealing
Hoarding
Isolating
Excessive sleeping

All addictions change our brain chemistry releasing chemicals that help soothe us, temporarily. The problem is when it wears off it can cause withdrawal-type symptoms which lead us right back to wanting the medication of the addiction, creating and Addiction Cycle. In time, we become powerless over this process. It takes an intervention of sorts, or moment of clarity, to break through this wall of denial. The first step is recognizing you might have a problem. The second step is being willing to do something about it.

Anger

Anger is essential in grieving. It may seem counterintuitive when thinking about grieving. Many of us have been shamed for feeling anger, especially women. Angry women aren't attractive. How many times have you heard, "She's a bitch" or "She just went crazy"? Women, traditionally, have learned to stifle their anger which leads to resentments that can take a long time to deal with in recovery. Stuffed anger can lead to eating disorders, shoplifting, and excessive shopping by women. It can sometimes be more difficult for men to identify their anger as a problem because they are often applauded for their "virile" expressions of anger. It's often considered more manly. But when the anger is chronic, explosive, (externally or internally), it is a sign that the grieving process is blocked. It needs to be examined, talked about, and released. In trauma healing, however, we often have to deal with rage.

Rage

One of the biggest blocks I've found over the years for dealing with grief is rage. I see rage as a combination of anger and shame inextricably bound together. If you have bouts of rage, such as out of control anger, excessive outbursts, or suicidal thoughts, it's time to deal with it. You need a safe person and place to start talking about your anger, a place where you won't be judged. The first time you start talking about your anger you may get loud and feel out of control which will trigger feelings of shame. It's important to keep talking about it, even though the shame will want you to stop. The more you talk about it the more you'll be able to just express it in a calm voice. This is very foreign to most survivors and takes practice. Remember, as survivors, we're dealing with the same thing even though we may come at in very different ways. The person who sits in silence, internalizing their rage is the same as the person who is vomiting their rage all over everybody. The silent rager thinks the verbal rager is a jerk and the verbal rager thinks the silent rager is a loser. They're just at opposite ends of the same spectrum. Sometimes it helps to visualize the rage and talk about what you see. I remember, years ago, watching the Watts riots. People were throwing large garbage cans through plate glass windows. I couldn't relate at all. I thought. "What's the matter with these people? Don't they have any self control?" Well, as my rage surfaced, that was the image that I kept seeing. I finally understood them. I would talk about how angry I was and felt like heaving a can through a window. After I'd expressed that image several times, I could finally just express the anger calmly. Shame, being a silent emotion, would release out of my body in the form of rashes, skin outbreaks, and other ailments. I'd "feel like a jerk". Waves of heat (shame) would escape my body. Sometimes I'd actually run a fever for a day. Little by little, step by step, I'd release the rage, the anger going one way, the shame, the other. I'd found a way to get out of the endless cycle and be free and at peace.

Bargaining

I call it the "If" cycle. "If only I'd done this," "If you would just do this, God, I promise to do better," "If You would just take me, and spare him". Anything not to feel the pain we're feeling, not to feel the loss, not to face the inevitability of the reality. Bargaining keeps us out of the present, the now. But being a stubborn creature I can bargain a long time trying to maintain an illusion of control. It usually takes me reaching exhaustion to stop bargaining and move to mourning or the more common label, depression.

Depression

This stage is all about sadness for me. I feel heavy, unmotivated, sometimes, immobile. It's also the stage that other people have the most problem with. They can't fix it so they try to fix you. How many times do you hear, "What's the matter with you?", "Smile, it can't be that bad." " Don't look so sad. You're making me feel sad." You know, like you're responsible for their feelings. It's so hard to be in this phase because it's so painful and you just want the pain to stop for a while. This is often when one relapses. The brain does not differentiate from one trauma to another or one pain from another. If you experience a trauma or pain, the brain connects with every other trauma you've ever experienced causing an overwhelming feeling of pain, helplessness, or vulnerability. That's why even a seemingly insignificant event can trigger overwhelming feelings of loss and sadness. It's important to feel the sadness, talk about it, and release the pressure of it, little by little, until you get to the other side of it.

This is also one of the reasons, I believe, why some people move through trauma and resolve it more quickly and easier than others. So if you're suffering from PTSD, quit shaming yourself and know that it's tied to other events and by working the steps you can untangle these traumas and let them go.

The creative arts can be very helpful during this stage of grieving. Music has always been important in my life. I've turned to it for as long as I can remember as a source of comfort, inspiration, and a sense of freedom. Listening to a sad song, I can connect with my own sadness, and often release it through tears I could not have otherwise shed. Studies have been done that show that when you cry out of emotion the tears have a different makeup. They contain hormones linked to stress, so a good cry releases stress and triggers the release of endorphins which is our body's natural medication for pain. Most people acknowledge they feel better after a good cry and now we know why. I have found that as long as I am acknowledging my grief in some way, I will get through it and be able to move on.

My world may look different. I may be different but I can reshape my views and rebuild my life.

During the intense years when I was retrieving and grieving deep abuse memories I began to put together a musical program which chronicled the grieving process I was going through. I performed it in treatment centers, at conferences for survivors and therapists alike. People would tell me how much I was helping people, which was great to hear, but every time I performed my program it helped and healed me too.

So think about what creative outlet you might turn to during your grieving process to help you through. Maybe it's time to get that guitar out of the back of your closet that you always said you were going to learn to play. Maybe it's time to take a dance or movement class. Or perhaps it's time to pack a lunch and go for a hike. Or maybe it's just time to be in fetal position and feel. Whatever you do, honor it and where you are in your process. Talk about where you are in your process and let the energy carry you through.

Acceptance

Eventually, I get to acceptance. It comes after mourning the loss or losses that occur when I finally speak my truth. Acceptance comes after I've expressed and felt all my emotions surrounding the trauma. I can't change what happened. I can't change what will happen. Everything happens for a reason and I may not know what that is right now but I can trust that I will be all right and that God has a purpose for it and me. Acceptance is finally being comfortable by myself. It's okay to be alone because in fact I'm never alone. God is with me.

It's in the surrender to God's will, not mine that true acceptance comes.

Step Eight

Made a list of all persons we had harmed and became willing to make amends to them all.

EXERCISE

My List:

Person   How did I harm them?

_____   _____

_____   _____

_____   _____

_____   _____

_____   _____

_____   _____

_____   _____

Lily Payton

Did I add myself to this list?

Am I willing to make amends to them all? If not, write the name(s) down.

_____

_____

_____

_____

_____

_____

Now, every day for two weeks, ask your Higher Power for the willingness to make amends. Then let it go.

Step Nine

Made direct amends wherever possible, except when to do so would injure them or others.

This step happens when it happens. It's important to discuss this with your sponsor to be sure you're not going to do more harm than good. It's very powerful to sit with someone and talk with them face to face about your past behaviors. Sometimes you can't locate someone, so you just have to be willing. Some people are no longer in this physical realm. I had to go to my father's grave and talk to him. Creating rituals are very powerful in healing work. Some people have done a ninth step years after they've worked the steps. Someone on their list shows up later in their life. There's no expiration date on this step.

Step Ten

*Continued to take personal inventory
and when we were wrong, promptly admitted it.*

This step is about daily vigilance. Once we have experienced trauma it gets imprinted in our cells. We are everything we have experienced; not only the story of the trauma, but the smells, sights, and sounds. Candace Pert explains this beautifully in her book, *Molecules Of Emotion*. Anything can trigger the memory, even if we've done the work. If I get triggered, I identify what the trigger is, what it's connected to, then release it. This brings me back to the opening of this book to explain why I ended up in the hospital in a blackout.

My husband and I went traveling for most of last year. I became lax in my spiritual program, went to only a few meetings the many months we were on the road. In October, we went under an overpass bridge on a small, rural road. We thought we had clearance but did not. The bridge shaved off the top of our RV. We drove to the nearest RV repair shop. They claimed it as a total loss. We couldn't afford to stay in a hotel so we lived in the trailer during the rain and cold. In the middle of the night the rain broke through the plastic barrier on the roof and drenched the bed. The carpets were wet and it turned into its own nightmare. We had to fight with our insurance claims department for three weeks to get decent reimbursement so we could get into a comparable vehicle. It seemed like it was never going to end. I did not realize how traumatized I was by it all.

Eventually, we got back on the road, only to have a blowout on the New Jersey turnpike. Believe me, your world does not feel safe standing on the side of the turnpike while your spare is being put on. The next incident happened in Tennessee. We were driving in the rain when my husband took an exit off the highway. The RV started swaying back and forth behind the truck. There was a steep embankment and I was sure we were going to tumble down it and die. He was able to bring it all under control, at the last minute, but I could not even speak for what seemed like forever. I didn't process any of this with anyone. I just stuffed it down. I was back in the attic crawlspace too terrified to speak.

When we got home to Texas, the adult me focused all that terror on finances. 'Cause that's what you do when you don't process trauma. You choose something, on a superficial level, to focus all your energy on and

Post Traumatic Stress Survivors Anonymous

channel all that terror into it. We had spent most of our money and when my husband didn't go to work right away when we got home I began to panic. Each day my fear grew worse, but I didn't say anything. I didn't speak up and tell my hus band how I was feeling. Instead, being in my victim, I felt like I had to handle it myself, that I was all alone, just like when I was trapped in the attic and the bathroom. So on that eventful Friday night, my husband was having a normal adult conversation with our RV landlord. They were talking about marriage and my husband responded to something our landlord said by saying, "Yea, I love being taken care of." The victimized child part of me became overwhelmed in that moment. I dissociated into the terror. I could not stay present. Even though I was walking and talking, I was at the same time trapped in my childhood trauma, feeling totally alone and responsible. No one was going to help me. There was no way out.

Stored trauma is very much like a backdraft in a fire. When firefighters are in a burning building, they are very careful when approaching a closed door. Often there is a build-up of toxic smoke and heat behind the door. If they open it quickly, introducing oxygen, it can cause an explosion of fire. Steps must be taken first to reduce the smoke and heat. That is why working the steps of the program are so important and probably why some are so resistant to doing them. The tenth step is all about reducing the trauma toxicity before it builds up. I was not processing my feelings each day (10th step work), building up the smoke and heat, if you will, creating increased pressure within me. I was not being honest. I was not keeping my world safe. The stress of frantically and continuously searching for a job I really didn't want to do, resulted in the oxygen that was introduced into this toxic environment creating an explosion in my mind resulting in the blackout.

I believe I was able to integrate because of all the previous work I had done. When I "came to" in that MRI machine, I was in the present and also simultaneously back in the original trauma of being confined in the attic crawl space. The panic and terror was overwhelming but I reached for my spiritual tools. I reached for help from my Higher Power. I completely and totally surrendered. In that instant, my brother who had locked me in that crawlspace, and who had died several years earlier, came to me spiritually. He reached his hand out to me and told me everything was okay. He told me to hold his hand, that I was not alone. All that old trauma was healed in that moment. The tears rolled down my face. A calm came over me and I finished the exam. All parts of me were integrated once again. I am so grateful that what my brother couldn't do for me in the physical realm he was able to do for me in the spiritual realm. It was definitely a fourth dimension experience.[*]

---

[*] *Alcoholics Anonymous*, pg. 25

This experience was humbling and an ego-squasher. After all my years of healing, I felt I was above and beyond my trauma. I had become spiritually arrogant. Today, I know I am all of who I am. Today, I embrace every part of me. I have a daily reprieve from my trauma contingent on my spiritual well-being.

Am I following my basic recovery rules?

Am I keeping my world safe on a daily basis?

Am I doing a daily inventory to see where I may have gone off track and if so, what steps am I taking to correct it?

Am I acting out any old negative survival skills?

Am I making a conscious contact with the God of my understanding on a daily basis?

It's a combination of going to the past (4th Step) along with changing present day behavior patterns (6th and 7th Step work) that break open the encapsulated traumas so you can release them and integrate them into your whole experience.

Step Eleven

Sought through prayer and meditation to improve our conscious contact with God, as we understood Him, praying only for knowledge of His will for us and the power to carry that out.

I didn't know where to begin with this step. It all seemed so foreign to me or contrived in a way much like my childhood faith had been to me. When I asked someone about it they said, "Well, praying is talking to God, and meditation is listening." That seemed like as good a place as any to start. Baby steps. That was the answer for this skeptic. Little by little, I was able to sit quietly and either pray or meditate.

This step grows deeper and more profound the more one works the steps. My contact with God began with the concept of the hologram and deepened to a personal one on one relationship with my own God. My spirituality grew and evolved because I took the advice of those who had gone before me in healing; I became open and willing to expand my consciousness.

Lily Payton

I experienced being, as the book *Alcoholics Anonymous* says, "rocketed into a fourth dimension of existence of which we had not even dreamed." A place beyond the three dimensional world, and deeper than words. This spiritual experience can be yours too, dive into the Steps and experience freedom, peace, and serenity.

Step Twelve

Having had a spiritual awakening as the result of these steps, we tried to carry this message to trauma survivors and to practice these principles in all our affairs.

Well, this brings me to now. I am stepping out in a public way, for the first time, to tell my story in the hopes that it might touch one troubled or tortured soul. To know you are not alone. To know you are not crazy. To find the courage to get with people of like minds and begin to really heal yourself, all of you, even the parts of you that have been hidden for so long. Bring all of you out into the light. Walk freely and proudly without fear or remorse.

If you have PTSD and it doesn't seem to be resolving, don't shame yourself. You're not weak or less than. It could very well be that your trauma is tied to childhood trauma that is buried deep within you, just like mine was. There's an expression, "The only way out is through." I had to retrace my history, go to my core, to release the stored trauma, bring it out of the repressed corners of my mind and cells of my body, to fully integrate and get free. Know that there is help. There is a solution. My vision is that there are Post Traumatic Stress Survivors Anonymous (PTSSA, I pronounce it like the word, pizza) meetings all over the world freely helping survivors of trauma.

Let me leave you with this Irish Prayer:

May God give you, for every storm, a
rainbow, For every tear, a smile,
For every care, a promise, And a blessing in each trial.
For every problem life sends, A faithful friend
to share, For every sigh, a sweet song,
And an answer for each prayer.

Suggested Reading

Alcoholics Anonymous World Services, Inc., *Alcoholics Anonyous* Fourth Edition, New York City.

Schaef, Anne Wilson, *Escape From Intimacy*, San Francisco: Harper & Row.

Schaef, Anne Wilson and Diane Fassel, *The Addictive Organization.*, San Fransisco: Harper & Row.

Schaeffer, Brenda, *Is It Love or Addiction: Falling Into Healthy Love*, New York: Harper & Row.

Sex and Love Addicts Anonymous, Boston: The Augustine Fellowship Press, 1986.

Siegel, Bernie, *Love, Medicine, and Miracles*, New York: Harper & Row.

Wholey, Denis, *The Courage to Change*, sold through Amazon.con

Woititz, Janet Geringer, *Struggle for Intimacy*, sold through Amazon.com

Carnes, Patrick, *Out of the Shadows: Understanding Sex Addiction*, Minneapolis: CompCare.

Gerber, Dr. Richard, *Vibrational Medicine*, Rochester, VT. Bear & Company.

Hay, Louise, *You Can Heal Your Life*, Santa Monica, CA: Hay House.

Beattie, Melodie, *Codependent No More*, New York, NY: Harper Collins Publishers.

Schaef, Anne Wilson, *Beyond Therapy, Beyond Science*, New York: Harper & Row.

Achterberg, Jeanne; Dossey, Barbara; Kolkmeier, Leslie, *Rituals of Healing*, New York, N.Y.: Bantam Books.

Talbot, Michael, *The Holographic Universe*, New York, N.Y.: Harper Collins Publishers.

Desjardins, Liliane, *The Imprint Journey*, Ann Arbor, MI: Loving Healing Press, 2012.

Pert, Candace B., *Molecules of Emotion*, New York, NY: Simon and Schuster, 1997.

Van der Kolk, Bessel A., *Psychological Trauma*, Washington, D.C.: American Psychiatric Press, Inc., 1987

I started and chaired a 12 twelve step meeting for trauma survivors for over a year. Here is the format of the meeting based on Alcoholics Anonymous 12 step meeting and additional info items that might be useful. Meetings last 1 hour. Start on time and end on time.

PTSSA THURSDAY EVENING MEETING

(Please edit this to fit your needs)

1. INTRODUCTION

Hi, my name is _____ and I am a trauma survivor. Welcome to the 5:30, Thursday meeting of Post Traumatic Stress Survivors Anonymous. At this time we ask that you silence your cell phones.

2. PREAMBLE:

PTSSA is a fellowship of men and women who share their experience, strength, and hope with each other that they may solve their common problem and help others to recover from stored trauma. The only requirement for membership is a desire to be free from trauma. There are no dues or fees for membership; we are self-supporting through our own contributions.We are not allied with any sect, denomination, politics, organization, or institution; do not wish to engage in any controversy, neither endorse nor oppose any causes. Our primary purpose is to relieve stored trauma and help others understand that they are not a disorder but a thriving survivor.

3. WELCOME

Is there anyone attending PTSSA for the first time? If so, please give us your first name so we can begin to know you better.

Is there anyone in their first 90 days of trauma (PTSSA) recovery?

Are there any visitors today, and if so, what brings you here today?

4. MEETING STATEMENT

PTSSA is a recovery program based on the book, "PTSD, A Way Up And Out" and the 12 steps and traditions modified from Alcoholics Anonymous. We acknowledge that stress can recreate symptoms we thought we had resolved or heighten existing symptoms. Therefore, we acknowledge spiritual progress not perfection. We take responsibility for our symptoms and actions. Trauma symptoms and triggers are posted. If you have found your way here you may be dealing with some of them. We do not tolerate shaming of any kind, either of self or others. We provide a safe, nurturing environment to heal and thrive and above all are gentle with ourselves and others at all times. We share our experience, strength, and hope with each other.

We are not therapists, We do not diagnose or treat. PTSSA is not a replacement for therapy or other professional services. We provide a program of recovery that suggests we work through the 12 steps with the help of another recovering trauma survivor. Our traumas do not define us. With the help of a Higher Power, as we understand it, and group support, we find we can live happy, healthy, free lives.

5. SERENITY PRAYER

At this time, let's have a few moments of silence followed by the Serenity Prayer:

> God, grant me the serenity to accept the things I cannot change, The courage to change the things I can And the wisdom to know the difference.

6. MEETING GUIDELINES

Our goal is to create a safe place in these rooms where each person's boundaries are respected. To ensure this:

1. Crosstalk is prohibited, meaning that we refrain from commenting on others' shares. We do not interrupt or give advice to another. We keep the focus on ourselves and share from the "I" position, not the "we" position.

2. We will go around the room, as time allows, to give all a chance to share. When we come to you, please introduce yourself by your first name. If you don't wish to share just say, "I'll pass."

3. Everything and everybody is held in strict

confidence. What you hear here, who you see here, let it stay here.

4. No one is to be touched while they are sharing even if your intentions are well meant. If you become uncomfortable during someone else's share, reflect on what step YOU'RE on at that moment. We save hugging for after the meeting, but only after getting permission.

5. Tissues are available for personal use. Help yourself as needed. Do not offer anyone tissues during their share.

We will now read the steps suggestive for trauma recovery:

1. We admitted we were powerless over our past traumas, that our lives had become unmanageable.

2. Came to believe that a Power greater than ourselves could restore us to sanity.

3. Made a decision to turn our will and our lives over to the care of God as we understood Him.

4. Made a searching and fearless moral inventory of ourselves.

5. Admitted to God, to ourselves, and to another human being the exact nature of our negative survival skills.

6. Were entirely ready to have God remove all these negative survival skills, one at a time.

7. Humbly asked Him to remove our negative survival skills.

8. Made a list of all persons we had harmed, and became willing to make amends to them all.

9. Made direct amends to such people wherever possible, except when to do so would injure them or others.

10. Continued to take personal inventory and when we were wrong promptly admitted it.

11. Sought through prayer and meditation to improve our conscious contact with God as we understood Him, praying only for knowledge of His will for us and the power to carry that out.

12. Having had a spiritual awakening as the result of these steps, we tried to carry this message to trauma survivors, and to practice these principles in all our affairs.

8. MEETING FORMAT

Our meeting is based on the 12 steps of trauma healing. We will work through the steps based on Lily Payton's book, Post Traumatic Stress Survivors Anonymous. We will read the step we are on and work through the exercises as time allows. After each exercise we will open it up for discussion.

(record on the sheet where we ended. This will be the starting point for the next meeting.)

Today we will be focusing on step _____.

(Read the step, do exercises if any, and open for discussion)

9. CLOSING

That is all the time we have for today. If you didn't get a chance to share, please talk to someone after the meeting.

Here at PTSSA we give chips to celebrate milestones in our recovery. While we're offering chips we will pass the basket and our service opportunity sheet for greeting, chairing, setting up, cleaning up

We are self-supporting through our own contributions. We ask that everyone give what they can, knowing that a dollar doesn't go very far these days, and we need to pay our rent. If you can't give, don't worry, we need you more than we need your money.

Please help be a part of and support the group by signing up for service opportunities.

(setting up if needed, cleaning up, and being a greeter.)

NOW:

Is there anyone celebrating 30 days of PTSSA recovery?

Anyone have 90 days?

6 months?

9 months?

1 year?

Multiple years?

10. LET'S CLOSE WITH THE SERENITY PRAYER.

FLYER

PTSSA MEETING

(Post Traumatic Stress Survivors Anonymous)

Do you suffer from any of these PTSD symptoms?

Nightmares, flashbacks, tremors, hypervigilance, startle response,

numbing out, emotional swings,

addictions, panic attacks, anxiety

And just when you think you've "licked it", your symptoms return to haunt you.

Come join us at PTSSA, and find a free, safe, environment to help heal from past traumas. This is a twelve step program where you can find a safe and supportive place to flourish and be free.

Meetings will be:
Date:
Day:
Time:
Place:

Be part of something from the very beginning. Help launch the first ever PTSSA meeting on _____.

Printed in the United States
By Bookmasters